D0826254

Stories

Penny King & Clare Roundhill

Artists' Workshop

Crabtree Publishing Company

350 Fifth Avenue
Suite 3308
New York, NY 10118

360 York Road, R.R.4
Niagara-on-the-Lake
Ontario L0S 1J0

73 Lime Walk
Headington, Oxford
England 0X3 7AD

Edited by **Bobbie Kalman**
Designed by **Jane Warring**
Illustrations by **Lindy Norton**
Children's pictures by
Amber Civardi, Charlotte Downham, Lara Haworth, Lucinda Howell, Sophie Johns, Julia Luther, Lucy MacDonald Watson, India Masson-Taylor, Zoë More O'Ferrall, Gussie Pownall, Thomas Stofer, Alice Williams, Jessica Williams
Photographs by **Peter Millard**
Picture Research **by Sara Elliott**

Created by
Thumbprint Books

Cataloging-in-Publication Data

Roundhill, Clare, 1964-
Stories/Clare Roundhill & Penny King.
p. cm. -- (Artists' workshop)
Includes index.
Summary: Presents six works of art each of which tells a story using a different technique. Includes instructions for using these techniques to make one's own pictures and stories.
ISBN 0-86505-852-0 (hc). -- ISBN 0-86505-862-8 (paper)
1. Art--Technique--Juvenile literature. [1. Art--Technique.]
I. King, Penny, 1963- . II. Title. III. Series.
N7433.R68 1996 702'.8--dc20 95-50854
CIP
AC

First published in 1996 by
A & C Black (Publishers) Limited
35 Bedford Row, London WC1R 4JH

Printed and bound in Singapore

Cover Photograph:
The Harvest, 1989, is a Peruvian *Arpillera* (appliqué).
Women throughout Latin America make embroidery pictures, like this, to tell stories about their life in villages and on farms. Women's organizations sell them to help raise money for their communities.

Contents

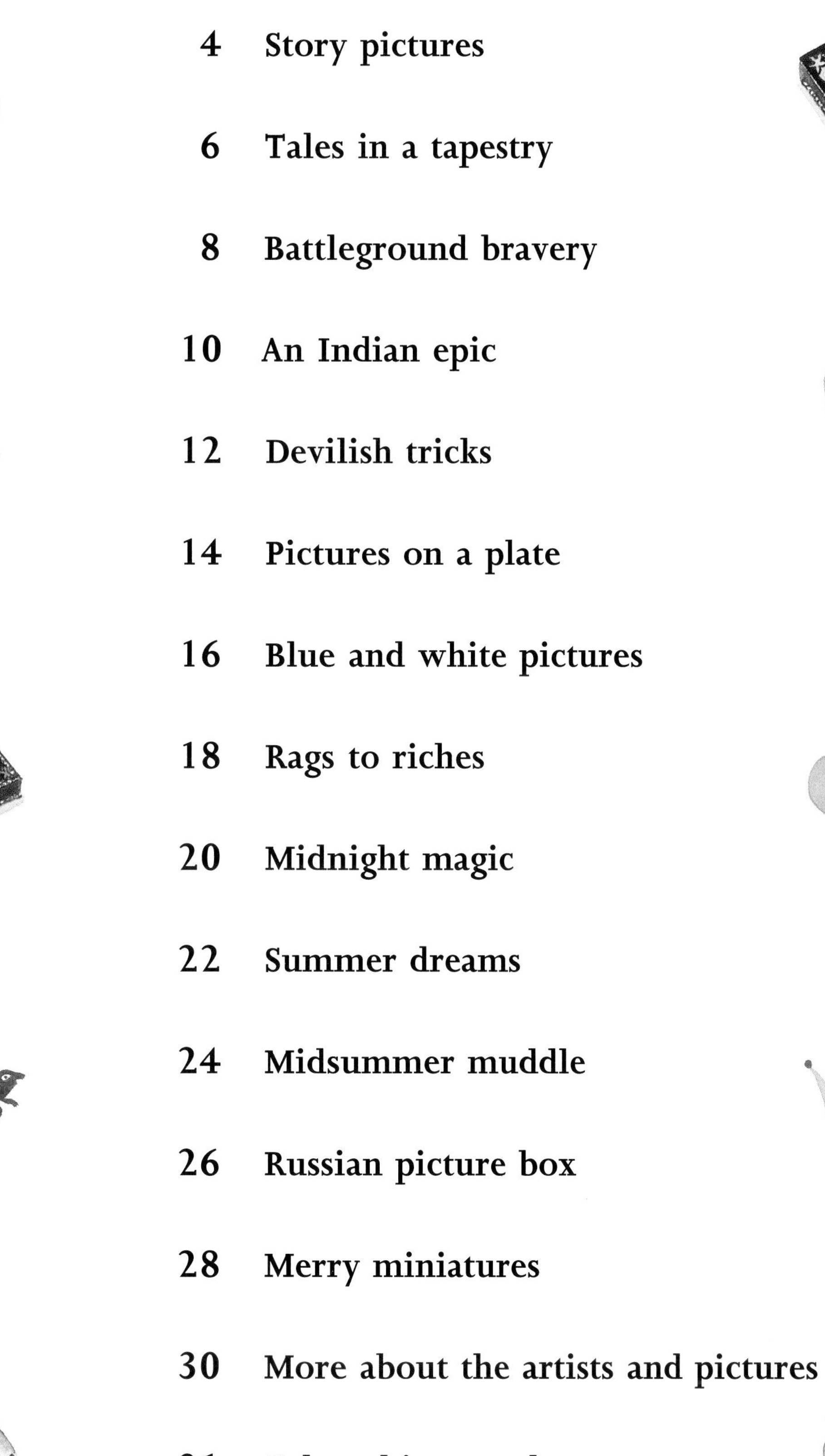

Story pictures

Long ago, most people did not learn to read and write. Instead, they listened to stories and learned about ideas and events from pictures or what other people told them.

The Ancient Greeks illustrated scenes from myths on vases and plates and carved the heroes in marble and wood.

In the Middle Ages, people in Europe were taught about the Bible through the stories carved in stone around the entrance to churches or on the stained-glass windows inside.

In India several hundred years ago, storytellers traveled from village to village with an illustrated scroll that unfolded to show scenes from great epics. In the East, epic stories were often performed as puppet plays.

In many cases, stories were illustrated on walls, rugs, tapestries, cups and plates and even on clothes. Today, you can read stories in books or watch them on television or film. All kinds of stories are also told in cartoons.

Ballets and operas also tell exciting stories. Music and mime help explain the plots, which are sometimes quite long and complicated.

Pictures can say as much, if not more, than words. The six main pictures in this book each tell a wonderful story. There is the embroidered story of a real battle that took place almost a thousand years ago; a Russian fairy tale about a frog princess and the brave prince who rescued her; a magical tale of love and confusion by Shakespeare; an ancient Indian saga about a royal prince and a wicked demon.

There is also the enchanting story of Cinderella and a fable painted on a plate.

You may find that the pictures that illustrate these stories don't match up with the ones you have in your head.

Use all the techniques shown in the book to illustrate your versions of these stories and then try creating pictures of your own favorite stories.

Tales in a tapestry

The Bayeux Tapestry was made over 900 years ago and is like a huge cartoon strip. The pictures embroidered on it tell the story of one of the most famous battles in history, called the Battle of Hastings, and all the events that led up to it. It was fought between King Harold of England and William, Duke of Normandy.

The Bayeux Tapestry 11th Century. By special permission of the City of Bayeux

The tapestry shows men hunting, farming, feasting, meeting friends and building ships and castles, as well as the two armies fighting fiercely. To protect themselves, the soldiers carry shields and wear chain-mail armor and helmets with long nosepieces.

This picture, near the end of the tapestry, shows the death of King Harold. Nobody knows whether Harold is the man with the arrow in his eye or the soldier being struck by a Norman knight. The border at the bottom shows men collecting weapons from dead soldiers.

The Bayeux Tapestry story

Long ago in England there lived a king called Edward the Confessor, who had no children to take his place when he died. Many people thought they had a right to become the next king. One of them was the King's cousin, William, Duke of Normandy. He claimed that Edward had promised him the throne.

Edward sent his brother-in-law, Harold, to meet William. The two powerful warriors became good friends, but when King Edward became ill, he called Harold back to England to help him rule.

When Edward died, Harold was crowned King of England. William was very angry because he felt that Harold had deceived him. He decided to fight Harold for the throne.

William loaded up boats with soldiers and horses and sailed to England to fight Harold at Hastings.

Harold and his men fought bravely, but they were no match for William's strong army. They were defeated, and Harold was killed. William became King of England on Christmas Day, 1066. From that day on, he was known as William the Conqueror.

Battleground bravery

The Bayeux Tapestry was sewn by skilled needlewomen who used many different stitches but only eight colors. It would probably take days, or even weeks, to draw all the people, animals and events it shows. Here are several different ways of making your own Bayeux-style pictures.

Stitched shield

Make a colored sketch of a shield like one of those used by the soldiers in the tapestry. Design a bold pattern or fancy initials for it, or draw a picture of a fierce animal to frighten away enemies. Stitch the outline of your shield on a square of felt. Sew the details in different-colored threads and stitches.

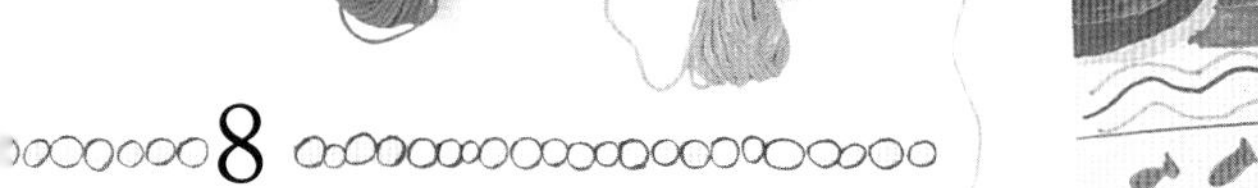

Colossal collage

Make a collage of a fierce battle scene. Use a large piece of pale felt for the background. Cut out soldiers with felt faces and shiny fabric armor. Stick on felt eyes and mouths and any other details. Use fleece or furry material for horses and stick on yarn for the manes and tales.

Glue everything onto the background and then add cocktail stick spears and flagpoles.

Story strip

Make your own comic strip of the Norman invasion. Cut two pieces of paper in half and glue the four strips together. Draw one part of the story on each strip with a decorated border along the top and bottom.

An Indian epic

Ramayana is a famous ancient Indian saga. Centuries ago, this long and exciting tale about Rama, a blue-skinned prince, was told by storytellers. In the 3rd century BC, a poet called Valmiki wrote it down. Later, the story was shown in exquisitely detailed pictures so that people who could not read could follow the tale.

Sanskrit illumination for the Ramayana. The British Library, London

There are over 400 pictures in the series from which this painting comes. Often, a team of artists worked years on illustrations for rich kings. The master artist sketched each drawing, and lesser artists filled in the colors.

This picture shows the part of the story when Rama is living in the forest. He is having a meal with his wife, Princess Sita, and his brother, Lakshmana. Bows and arrows hang on the hut ready for the two princes to go out hunting for deer.

Rama's story

A long time ago, in India, there lived a prince, called Rama. His jealous stepmother had him banished because she wanted her own son to be the next king. For 14 years, Rama lived deep in the forest with his wife, Princess Sita, and his brother, Lakshmana.

One day an evil ten-headed demon, called Ravana, sent a golden deer to lure Prince Rama away from Sita.

Ravana kidnapped the princess and flew off with her in his chariot. On the way to the demon's palace on the island of Lanka, Sita threw out her jewels, hoping that Rama would find them and come to rescue her.

Rama and Lakshmana searched all over India until they came to the land of the monkeys. They made friends with Hanuman, the monkey leader, who found Sita's jewels and told Rama where she was being held captive.

With the help of the monkeys, Rama and Lakshmana built a bridge across the dangerous sea and marched to Lanka. After days and nights of fierce battle, Rama killed Ravana and rescued his faithful Princess Sita.

At last, it was time for Rama to return home and take his place as king. His loyal subjects lit hundreds of oil lamps to guide their hero back to his kingdom.

Devilish tricks

Imagine what Ravana, the evil demon, looked like and then create one or all of his ten ugly heads. You might like to paint or print a delicately patterned picture of the part of Prince Rama's story that you enjoyed the most.

Ugly Ravana

Draw the outline of one of Ravana's ugly heads on a piece of stiff cardboard. Mix a sickly shade of green poster paint and add some flour to make it really thick. Paint the head with the mixture and let it dry.

Paint or glue hideous features onto the face. You could use scrunched-up tissue paper for eyes, a toilet-paper roll for the nose, a sponge for a lolling tongue, silver foil for horns and black yarn for hair. Paint the eyes, nose and mouth.

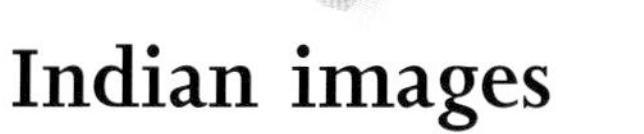

Indian images

Use felt-tipped pens, paints or crayons to illustrate any part of Prince Rama's story. Fill the paper with bright colors, busy figures and animals. Use lots of delicate patterns for the leaves, clothes and flowers.

Printed princess

Collect several different items for making prints, such as a cork, sponge, tea towel, potatoes or cauliflower florets cut in half. Using poster paints, practice printing with each one to see what different shapes and textures they make.

Now create a printed picture—maybe of Princess Sita in a beautiful dress wearing her jewels or the furry monkeys helping Rama build the bridge. When the paint is dry, outline the figures in black.

Pictures on a plate

The pattern on this plate looks Chinese, but it was first made in England. It is one of the best-known designs in the world and is called the 'willow pattern'. If you look closely, you can see the pictures that tell a very sad Chinese story.

Spode willow pattern plate, about 1790, by courtesy of Spode, Stoke-on-Trent

The Chinese were the first people to paint patterns on porcelain in this color, cobalt blue. When this plate was made, Chinese art was very fashionable in Europe. Many factories, including Spode in England, copied Chinese designs and put them onto plates, bowls and dishes, using transfers.

The willow pattern was based on a Chinese design that showed a beautiful landscape. To make it more interesting, Josiah Spode added the long fence and the three people going over the bridge. Several people looked at the willow pattern and made up their own stories to fit the pictures.

The willow pattern story

A long time ago in China, there lived a rich man called T'so Ling, who had a beautiful daughter, Koong Shee. Although they lived in a magnificent palace with wonderful gardens, Koong Shee was very lonely. Her only friend was the gardener, Chang. The two soon fell in love.

When Koong Shee's father found out about them, he was very angry and sent Chang away forever. He arranged for Koong Shee to marry a rich old man, and he locked her in a small house from which there was no escape. Every day her tears fell into the river like the leaves from the nearby weeping willow tree.

On the night before her wedding, Chang arrived in a boat. He and Koong Shee ran away, taking with them a big box of jewels. Koong Shee's father chased them over a bridge, but the lovers ran too fast for him and managed to escape.

For many years, they lived happily on a nearby island until, one day, Koong Shee's father discovered them. He threw them into a dark maze, where they died.

The gods knew how much Koong Shee and Chang had loved each other. They turned their spirits into a pair of doves so they could fly together forever above the weeping willow tree.

Blue and white pictures

Imagine that you have entered the blue and white world of the willow pattern. Use the ideas of the story about Koong Shee, or make up your own, to create a plate painted with pictures and patterns.

Painted plates

Decide which parts of the willow pattern story you want to show and then draw them in pencil on a white cardboard circle. Draw a patterned border around the edge.

Put blue and white paint onto a palette or into two separate pots. Mix a little of each in different amounts to make different shades of blue. The more white you add, the paler the blue will become. Paint your story using a fine-tipped paintbrush so you can put in lots of details and patterns.

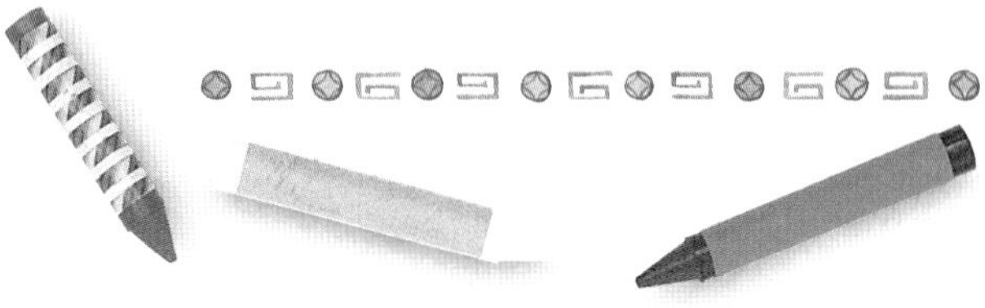

Willow-wax wash

With a dark blue wax crayon, draw your favorite part of the willow pattern story on a sheet of paper. Mix a little pale blue paint with water. Brush it all over the picture. The wax picture will shine through the paint.

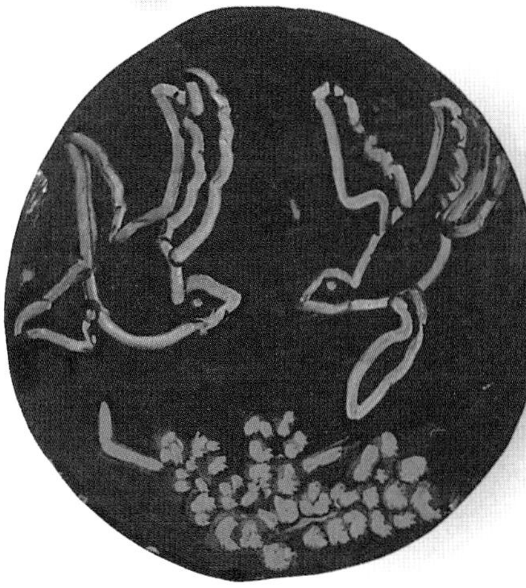

Black and blue

Cover a white cardboard circle with a thick layer of blue poster paint and leave it to dry. When you are sure it is dry, cover the blue paint with a thick layer of dark blue paint. While the dark blue paint is still wet, use a cotton swab to draw a scene from the willow pattern story.

Rags to riches

This illustration of Cinderella is by an English artist called Arthur Rackham. He became famous for his illustrations of fairy tales and children's stories.

Arthur Rackham illustration for Cinderella by C.S. Evans, 1919

Early in the 1900s, when Rackham painted this illustration, color printing had only recently been invented. Color pictures were printed on shiny paper, separately from the pages of the story. They were stuck into the books by hand.

Rackham used four main colors—brown, black, green and red—to show how sad Cinderella is feeling. Since she is the main character, she is painted in great detail. Everyone else is painted as a black shape, known as a silhouette.

The story of Cinderella

There was once a beautiful girl called Cinderella who lived with her father, her cruel stepmother and two unkind stepsisters. All day long, she cooked and cleaned for them, dressed in rags and ate only scraps, but she never once complained.

One day, an invitation came for everyone in the house to attend the king's ball. Poor Cinderella was not allowed to go. She was forced to spend every spare minute sewing her ugly sisters' new ballgowns. On the day of the event, her excited sisters got ready and went off to the ball in a fine coach.

Cinderella sat crying by the fire, wishing she could go to the ball, too. All of a sudden, her fairy godmother appeared. With a swish of her magic wand, she turned a pumpkin into a coach, mice into horses, and gave Cinderella a beautiful silver dress with a pair of fine sparkling slippers. She told Cinderella to be home by midnight, when the spell would wear off.

When Cinderella arrived at the ball, no one knew who she was. The Prince fell in love with her immediately and danced with her all night. When the clock struck twelve, however, Cinderella rushed out of the ballroom, dropping one of her slippers on the palace steps. The Prince took the slipper to every house in the land to find its owner. When he came to Cinderella's house, the ugly sisters rushed to try on the slipper, but it was too small for them. Cinderella's foot, however, was a perfect fit. The happy prince asked her to marry him, and she did.

Midnight magic

Create your own illustrations to go with the story of Cinderella. Once you have tried the different techniques, you might like to use all three together, as Rackham did, to make one incredible picture.

Handsome prints

Choose a simple shape from the story, such as a glass slipper, a mouse or a royal crown. Practice drawing it until you have a strong, realistic outline.

With a black felt-tipped pen, draw this shape on a thin, flat sponge and then carefully cut it out. Glue it onto a square piece of cardboard. Let the glue dry before you start printing.

Dampen the sponge shape and cover it with poster paint. Press it, paint face down, onto brightly colored bristol board. Repeat this until you have a page covered with prints.

Shadow play

Using white chalk, draw the outlines of Cinderella and the other characters on black cardboard.

Carefully cut out the figures and arrange them on a sheet of white paper. Glue them in position, chalky side down. Add details, such as a hat, a pair of gloves or a bow, in different-colored cardboard.

Hopes and dreams

In his picture, Rackham has made Cinderella look sad because she could not go to the ball. He has chosen sad, dark colors that match her miserable mood.

Think about the colors that best match each part of the story. They could be bright and sparkling for the moment when the prince finds Cinderella, clashing for the two ugly sisters, or pale for Cinderella's moonlit dash to the ball.

Paint a picture in which the figures tell the story and the colors describe the mood.

Summer dreams

Marc Chagall was a Russian artist, but he spent much of his life traveling and working in France. He often used the memories of his childhood, mixed with dreams and Russian folklore, to create his exotic pictures, mosaics, stained-glass windows and intricate tapestries.

Marc Chagall, Midsummer Night's Dream, 1939, Musée de Grenoble

This painting was inspired by a play called 'A Midsummer Night's Dream'. It was written about 400 years ago by William Shakespeare, the most famous English playwright.

Chagall liked the play so much that he read it over and over again. The picture shows beautiful Queen Titania and her lover, Bottom. He was a man with a donkey's head.

The story of 'A Midsummer Night's Dream'

Deep in an enchanted wood lived Oberon, King of the fairies, and his beautiful Queen, Titania. One day, King Oberon decided to play a cruel trick on Titania because she had quarrelled with him.

While Titania slept, the King squeezed magic juice on her eyelids. This made her fall in love with the first thing she saw when she woke up—a man, called Bottom, who had been given a donkey's head by Puck.

As Titania lovingly stroked Bottom's furry face, two lovers, called Hermia and Lysander, ran past her into the woods. They were being chased by Demetrius, who wanted to marry Hermia. Close behind Demetrius came Helena, who loved Demetrius dearly, though he did not love her!

Seeing them all in such a muddle, King Oberon ordered his helper, Puck, to drop the magic juice into Demetrius's eyes so that he might fall in love with Helena. By mistake, Puck put the drops into Lysander's eyes instead. Quickly, the King charmed Demetrius's eyes as well, and soon both men were hopelessly in love with Helena.

Taking pity on the lovers, King Oberon took the spell off young Lysander, who immediately fell back in love with Hermia, leaving Helena to Demetrius. The king also removed the charm from Titania's eyes, and she became his loving Queen once more.

Midsummer muddle

In many of his paintings, Chagall used unrealistic colors and bold shapes. He often showed people and objects floating in the air. Why not let your imagination take over and help you create your own dream pictures?

Slumbering Titania

On white paper, draw a picture in pencil of Titania asleep in her bed of flowers or Hermia and Lysander running away through the woods. Use simple but bold shapes crowded together to give your picture the feeling of a dream.

Wet the paper all over with a paintbrush dipped in water. Dip a fountain pen into India ink and trace over your pencil outlines.

When the paper is dry, paint your picture with pale watercolors. It doesn't matter if the colors go over the lines. The more smudged and blurred your painting is, the more unusual and dreamlike it will look.

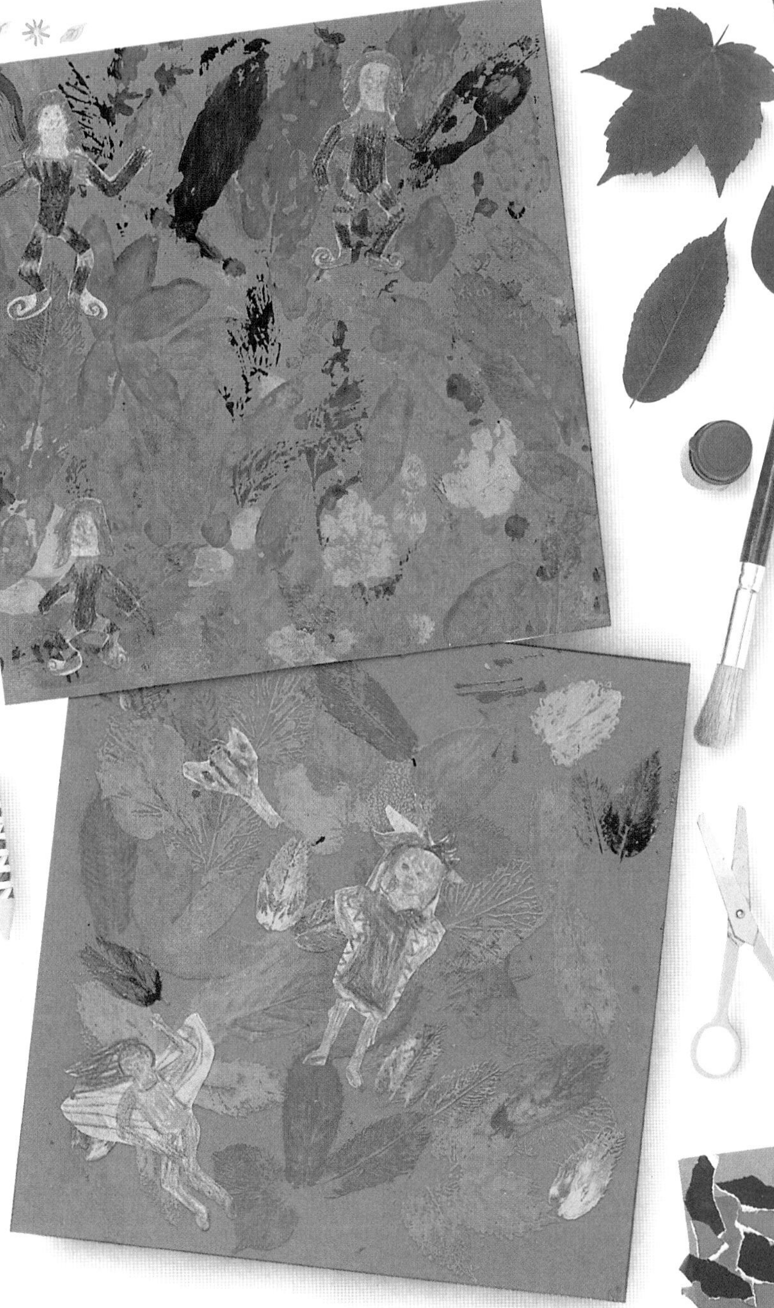

Fairy glade

Collect leaves of different shapes and sizes. Paint the veined side of each leaf a different shade of brown or green. Before they dry, press the painted leaves onto a big sheet of paper. Let the leaf prints dry.

Draw some fairies on tracing paper and color them with wax crayons, using the same colors that you used for the leaves. Cut them out and glue them onto the leafy background.

Fuzzy feelings

Sketch one of the scenes from 'A Midsummer Night's Dream' and then draw your picture on the back of colored paper. Instead of cutting out the shapes, carefully tear along the pencil outlines.

Glue the shapes onto a colorful sheet of paper. The torn edges will give your picture a slightly fuzzy and dreamy look.

Russian picture box

The tiny picture on this papier mâché box was painted by a Russian artist, called Yagodkina. It shows part of a Russian folktale, which tells the story of Prince Ivan, his frog princess and the evil Kaschey.

Yagodkina, Russian Miniature Box, 1992, Iconastas, London

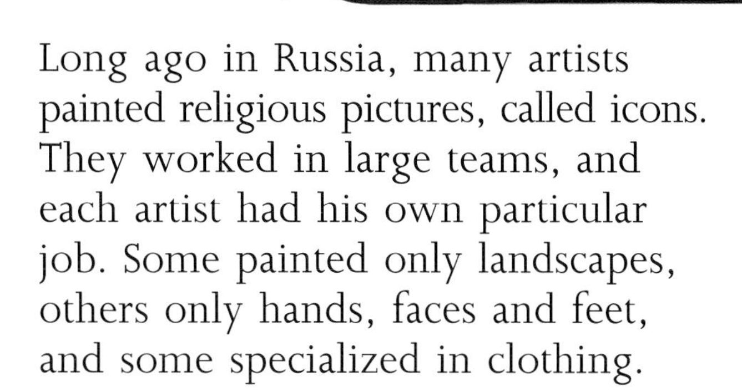

Long ago in Russia, many artists painted religious pictures, called icons. They worked in large teams, and each artist had his own particular job. Some painted only landscapes, others only hands, faces and feet, and some specialized in clothing.

Later, religious worship was forbidden in Russia. Instead of painting icons, artists began to decorate wood, metal and pottery with pictures based on folktales, songs and history. One artist was allowed to paint a whole picture instead of just a part of it.

The story of the frog princess

An old Tsar once had three sons. When it was time for them to marry, he told each one to shoot an arrow into the air. Wherever their arrows fell, they would find a wife. Ivan, the youngest prince, was disgusted to find a frog beside his arrow, but he was forced to marry her.

The Tsar held a ball to celebrate the weddings. Prince Ivan waited for his frog princess to arrive, but to his surprise, a beautiful girl appeared instead. She explained that her father had cast a spell on her so that she had to spend most of her time as a frog, but soon the spell would wear off. When Prince Ivan got home, he found her discarded frog skin on the floor and quickly burned it. The princess was horrified. Now her father's spell would never be broken. She had to leave for the faraway kingdom of the evil Kaschey.

The prince searched high and low for his princess until he met an old witch who told him that Kaschey lived beneath a huge oak tree. The only way to kill him was to break a needle found in an egg. On his way, Prince Ivan met a bear, a hare, a duck and a big fish. Each, in turn, begged him not to kill them. They promised that, in return, they would help him one day.

Ivan found the tree and wondered how to reach Kaschey. Suddenly, the bear rushed up and knocked the tree over. A stone chest fell from its branches and smashed. The hare popped out of the chest, fell down, and died. The duck flew out of the dead hare and dropped an egg into the sea. Ivan wept when he realized that the needle must be inside the egg. All at once, the fish rose out of the waves with the egg in its mouth. Ivan grabbed it and snapped the needle inside. Kaschey died instantly. The spell was broken. Ivan and his wife lived happily ever after.

Merry miniatures

Yagodkina used fine detail and intricate patterns when she painted the picture on her box. You can try to do the same or you could decorate a bigger box with characters cut out of patterned paper instead.

Shiny picture box

Cover a box with a thick layer of black poster paint. While it is drying, make a simple sketch of one of the characters from the frog princess story, such as Prince Ivan or the duck.

Cut the shapes you need out of patterned paper and shiny candy wrappers. Arrange them on top of the black box and then carefully glue the pieces down.

Painted box

Cover a small box with two thick layers of black poster paint. Use a fine brush to paint a delicate and detailed picture of your favorite character from the story.

When the paint is dry, use a gold felt-tipped pen to create a border around your picture and add details.

Precious paintings

With bright poster paints and a fine brush, paint a picture from the frog princess story on some black paper. Use as many colors as you like. Let the paint dry.

With a fine gold or silver felt-tipped pen, make a patterned frame around your picture. Add details, such as delicate leaves, lattice windows or soft fur.

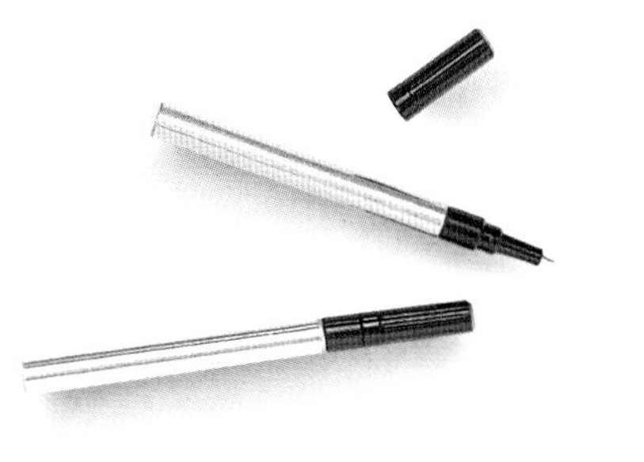

Nesting animals

Cut a long strip of white paper and fold it into five equal parts. Paint a chest on the first space, making sure that its sides touch the edge of the paper and the first fold. In the next space, draw a hare with its nose touching the chest and its bottom on the second fold.

In the same way, draw a duck, an egg and a needle in the last three spaces. Color the pictures with felt-tipped pens. Carefully cut them out, leaving them attached to each other. You now have a strip of pictures that fold one under the other.

More about the artists and pictures

The Bayeux Tapestry
(Late 11th Century)

Many people think that Bishop Odo, King William's half-brother, ordered the Bayeux tapestry to be made. He hung it in his cathedral at Bayeux for everyone to see at festivals and on special occasions. It remained there for several centuries before being seized during the French Revolution and taken to Paris. Now it is back in Bayeux in its own museum. The end of the tapestry seems to have been lost. It would probably have shown William being crowned King of England.

The Ramayana

(Mid 17th Century)

The illustration of Prince Rama, Princess Sita and Lakshmana comes from the Ayodhyakanda, or second book of the Ramayana. It tells of the life of Rama and Sita in the forest and was completed in Udaipur in 1650. No one knows who painted the 68 pictures in the book, but they are likely to be from the studio of Sahib Din. He would probably have sketched the detailed pictures and allowed assistants to color them in.

The Willow Pattern
(1790)

Although nobody really knows who the artist of the willow pattern was, Thomas Minton may have made the original engraving. He was a fine craftsman who worked for Spode for ten years before setting up his own pottery. At that time, Chinese porcelain was popular in Europe and when, in 1784, tea became cheaper to buy, Spode began to produce Chinese-style tea sets. Because they were made in England, they were much cheaper than those shipped all the way from China.

Cinderella

(1919)
Arthur Rackham 1867 - 1939

Arthur Rackham worked as a clerk in a fire station before he became an artist. He became well known for his delicate pictures of children, fairies, and trees that looked almost human. Among the many books he illustrated were Peter Pan, Alice in Wonderland and the fairy tales of Hans Christian Anderson and The Grimm Brothers. At the age of seventy he illustrated his last book—The Wind in the Willows.

Midsummer Night's Dream
(1939)
Marc Chagall 1887 - 1985

As well as painting pictures, Chagall loved working on large stage sets and designing costumes for the theatre and ballet. The artist, who was a Jew, spent two years working on twelve stained-glass windows for the synagogue at the Hadassah-Hebrew University in Jerusalem. He also designed three huge tapestries to hang on the walls of the Israeli Parliament and painted enormous panels for the ceiling of the Paris Opera House.

Russian Miniature Box
(1992)

Yagodkina

Yagodkina lives in the town of Palekh, in Russia, where icon painters have worked since the 12th century. Today their miniatures, most of which are painted by women, are sold all over the world. The artist took ten days to paint the picture on the box. She used a fine paintbrush with only four hairs so that she could paint the intricate details. When she was finished, she covered the box with seven layers of lacquer.

Other things to do

1 Cut out a cardboard circle and decorate it with stickers. Cut some big white cardboard petals. On each one, paint an exciting or important event that has happened to you. Start with the day you were born. Stick the petals, in order, clockwise around the center of the flower so that they tell your life story.

2 Design an information poster without any words, so that it could be understood by people all over the world. You could explain the safe way to cross a road, how to look after pets, or why it is important to brush your teeth every day. Draw several pictures to get your message across clearly.

3 Choose one of your favorite stories or make up a tale of your own. Try to tell it in one picture, similar to the willow pattern story. Include pictures of the setting and characters in the story. You might want to draw your story onto a paper plate and decorate the edge with a patterned border.

4 Create your own storybook by putting eight strips of paper one on top of the other. Fold them in half and sew them together along the fold. Write part of the story on each page. Illustrate the stories, using a different technique for each page, such as paint, silhouette and collage. Design an eye-catching cover.

Index

Acknowledgements
The publishers are grateful to the following institutes and individuals for permission to reproduce the illustrations on the pages mentioned.
The Harvest, 1989, Peruvian Arpillera, kindly lent by Sandy Adirondack: cover; The Bayeux Tapestry - 11th Century. By special permission of the City of Bayeux: 6; Sanskrit illumination for the Ramayana, The British Library, London (15296F.71r): 10; Spode willow pattern plate, by courtesy of Spode, Stoke-on-Trent: 14; Marc Chagall, Midsummer Night's Dream, 1939, Musée de Grenoble / © ADAGP, Paris and DACS, London, 1996: 22; Yagodkina, Russian Miniature Box, 1992, Iconastas, London: 26.

234567890 Printed in Singapore 6543210987